Behind the Grease Paint

A Clown's Chronicle in Vietnam

August 17, 2001

Dearest Arden -

This book is a reflection of your caring for others. You are a wonderful light in the world.

Thank you for the experiences and your friendship -

With my love -

Jill

Published by
Hara Publishing Group
P.O. Box 19732
Seattle, Washington 98109
(425) 775-7868

First printing, August 2001

ISBN: 1-883697-65-4
Library of Congress Number: 2001092729

Printed in USA
10 9 8 6 5 4 3 2

Cover Design: Jed Selter
Cover Photograph: Jed Selter
Book Design: Lisa Delaney

Behind the Grease Paint

A Clown's Chronicle in Vietnam

Jed Selter
Duffy the Clown

Hara
Publishing

Contents

Foreword

I have known Jed Selter for many years. This is by far the finest writing that he has shared. Jed has this passion, this significant quest that he is on. It is as if his journey is to pull in as much of life as he can and capture it in his own unique way to share with us as readers.

The one thing that is crystal clear in the writings of Jed Selter is his gift to translate his impressions from sights, sounds and human connections into images his readers can identify with, enjoy and embrace.

Jed's written words expose him for what he is all about. You cannot but help love the unique artistry he conveys. He lures you in to touch the visions and experiences registered in his memories. His words are about the uncompromising truth of life experiences: the beauty, the rawness and the tragedies which abound the roads, rivers and fields that he travels, painted by him in emotional shapes and colors.

Through his clowning, just one of his "give backs to Life," Jed summons up a component of relationship beyond the norm. It is not about the façade of his clown persona, but about cementing deep human connections far below the surface of verbal language and cultural differences.

Jed has a huge passion for Life, and, more importantly, to share beyond himself with and for others.

For those of you who are about to read Jed's works for the first time, clear your mind, open yourself, and be ready to laugh, cry and lust for the life passion that Jed puts down on paper. Embrace, as I have, this man's journey.

Dennis Broughton

Introduction

This short compilation of verses is a sub element of a work in progress I am entitling *Inside**Out**—A Book of Life's Experiences in Verse* which I intend to publish after two years of reflection and writing.

This book, *Behind the Grease Paint—A Clown's Chronicle In Vietnam*, is the second short book of verses to be part of my end result. The first recounts my feeling and experiences klowning in Hong Kong in December of 2000. It is entitled *Bring In The Klowns.*

The BMA Klown Klub

For more than twenty-five years, I have been a "klown" (as we spell it) in the Boeing Management Association (BMA) Klown Klub. The Klub is a nonprofit organization made up mostly of managers and sponsored by BMA. BMA itself is a nonprofit organization of managers from Boeing.

Our Klub charter is to klown in the local community. We klown at Special Olympics events, the Children's Hospital, with disabled youth and adults at various schools and functions, at Children's Protective Service parties, at retirement centers, and at Boeing organization open houses, picnics, and other events. We've been known to klown in local community celebration parades as well. Any money given to us is donated to Children's Hospital.

The Klub has been ongoing for approximately fifty years, and is considered an outstanding Boeing related community institution in the Seattle area. We are known as ambassadors of Boeing—even though the Klub is not officially sponsored by the Boeing Company.

There are presently twelve active Klowns. Each of us has learned klowning informally, mostly from each other—although I must say, we are very professional.

My klown name ("handle") is "Duffy." Since I spent years managing Boeing's Security and Fire Protection organizations, including the uniformed security officer corps, I was, until recently, "Duffy the Keystone Kop Klown," outfitted in a complete Keystone Cop costume.

Much of that costume has been passed down among three Klowns. The hat, an authentic English Bobby's hat, is over eighty years old.

Vietnam

In mid February to early March 2001, for two weeks, I traveled to Vietnam with a humanitarian nonprofit group called Kids First. This is a local group that raises money to help orphaned children, kids maimed by land mines, and those disfigured from the effects of Agent Orange, now in its third generation of harming Vietnamese children. Since I did not want to project a "law enforcement" clown persona in Vietnam, I changed my clown costume to a more generic clown image, with a vested double breasted jacket with "formal tails," striped jersey, red suspenders, a multi-colored two brimmed hat, green baggy knickers and bright yellow knee socks. I have shortened my "handle" to just plain "Duffy."

There were four of us who went as clowns on this trip: Don "Scooter" Hill, who first organized the clown contingent two years ago for Kids First, Mike "Safari" Keesling, who went last year with Scooter, and Lois "Tootie" Kerr, who also blazed the trail clowning in Vietnam last year with Scooter and Safari. Tootie is also a member of the BMA Klown Klub.

We traveled from the south of Vietnam, starting in Saigon, north to Hanoi. Along the route, we "worked" in towns, schools, orphanages and hospitals clowning. We were in Saigon, Hue, Dong Ha, Hoi An, Hai Phong and Hanoi.

For those of you who were there and experienced this first hand, please allow me "author's license" of events I have described. Some of this may not be technically accurate. But, this book is about passions, connections and emotions more than complete or factual accuracies.

To Roger and Nancy, Arden and Ben, Lam and Rand, core to Kids First—thank you for the experience of a lifetime. To the rest of the entourage who went, thank you for enriching me and letting me in with you.

To Scooter, Safari and Tootie, you know how I feel.

To Tim Alsberg, Dennis Broughton and Eric Greenwood—thank you for your friendship and your support on this verses project.

Lastly, to Lisa Delaney, who without hesitation contributed her extensive talent, her energy, and her time to the design of this book; and to Sheryn Hara, my publisher and my friend, for so caringly donating her efforts and her organization to publishing and distributing this work—thank you.

I am indebted to all of you.

Jed "Duffy" Selter
April 2001

Kids First Vietnam Trip

February 16-March 2, 2001

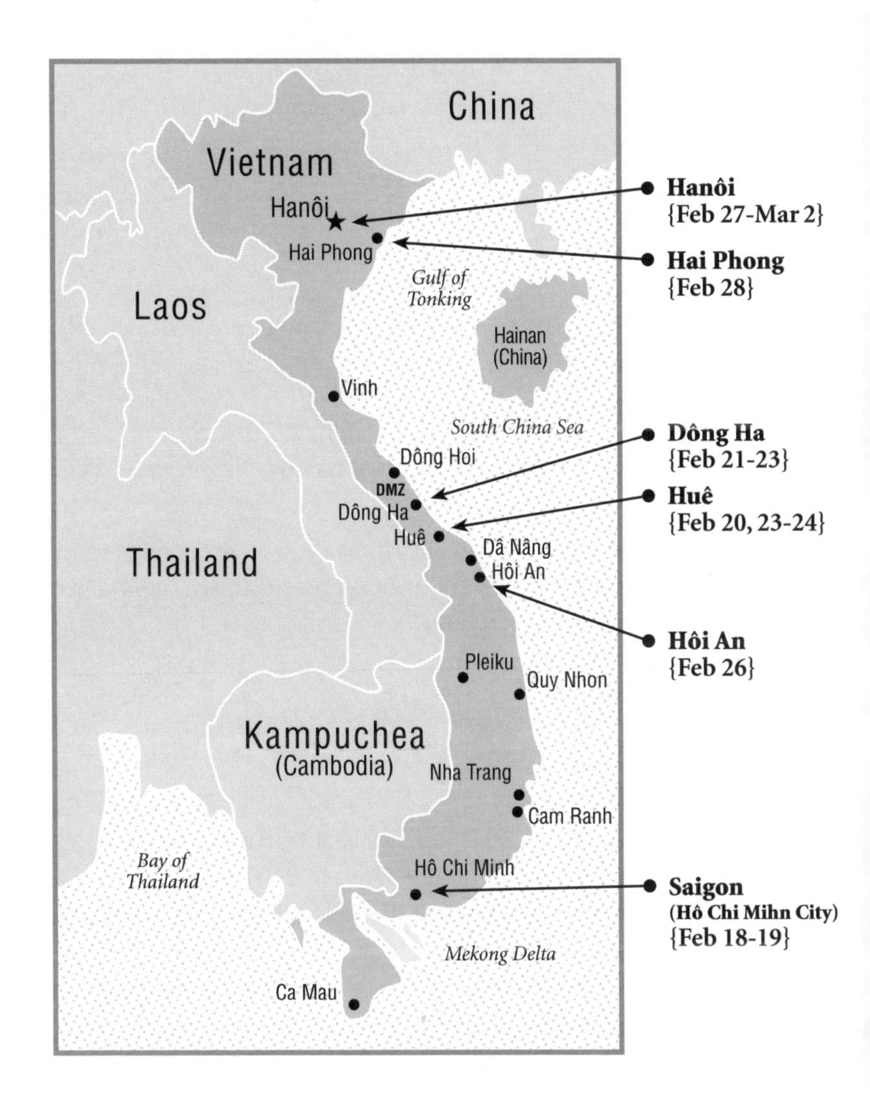

Kids First

Arden Norvold and Roger Ferrell are Co-Directors of Kids First Education Project, Vietnam, a nonprofit 501 (c) 3 humanitarian organization.

In 2000, Kids First provided scholarships for 350 handicapped and poor children of Dong Ha, Quang Tri Province, Vietnam. This is considered the poorest province in Vietnam, due to effects of Agent Orange, wartime carpet bombings, landmines, and unexploded ordnance left in the region.

Many children are handicapped due to third generation birth defects of Agent Orange and are victims of landmines and other explosives.

In 2000, solely with private donations, Kids First built the first handicapped accessible schoolhouse in Vietnam. It now educates 800 children who before had no schooling.

Kids First is presently building a world class and first of its kind in Vietnam Handicapped Rehabilitation Center/ Village in Dong Ha Town. Land mine clearing and construction for the Village's fifty-plus acre site is underway. It is scheduled to open in 2003.

Kids First, operating since 1997, is fully supported by the United States Ambassador to Vietnam, The Honorable "Pete" Peterson.

If you are interested in supporting Kids First, your donations are tax deductible.

Arden Norvold and Roger Ferrell

You may reach Kids First at:

Kids First
PO Box 11814
Bainbridge Island, WA 98110

Roger Ferrell, Co-Director
Phone: (206) 780-4998
Email: rogerf@seanet.com.

Arden Norvold, Co-Director
Phone: (206) 612-2781
Email: anorvold@aol.com

Mixed Emotions

I had wanted this trip,
Had committed to it a year earlier.

Two weeks.
Twelve thousand miles away,
from Seattle to Vietnam.

I wanted it—cost and all.

She agreed, immediately.
If I wanted it, it was mine.
(She smiled.)

Beneath, I felt her hesitation,
But, she bade me "Yes, go."

Selfless to me—for me.
Hardship for her.

Work, home, dog.
What the two of us manage daily,
She will do alone.

On the reverse, I am excited to go.

A new experience with children,
With impassioned people I will
get to know and appreciate.

Exciting—but I worry about her.

I love her.

The Beginning

I assumed this trip would start
when we reached Saigon,
After twenty hours traveling.

I thought these relationships would
build slowly over days
From our real time experiences together.

But, I was wrong.

We were gathered in the private waiting
room at the airport,
Just chatting and milling around.

Somehow (I didn't see it happen)
We were in a large circle
all holding hands.
(People I had not yet met!)

And, then, in unison, people who
knew it, recited it...

"The light of God surrounds us,
The love of God enfolds us,
The power of God protects us,
The presence of God watches over us.
Wherever we are, God is,
And all is well."

Not a religious rite,
But a spiritual affirmation.

The energy surge was like a bolt of
electricity whipping around
that circle.

We held—fingers in fingers
As each introduced ourselves to the circle.

We broke our grasps,
All spontaneously clapping.

Headed to the departure gate,
Chit chatting along the way.

But, to me, feelings were deeper,
Connections already cementing.

The Universe at work, I told myself.
I know it.

Preparing us each for contributions not
yet in focus,
To be made in twenty plus hours time.

Many Have Come With Me

In the frenetic days packing for this
trip of a lifetime,
I took peaceful moments to focus.

To store up my essence,
A generator of energy for giving
unequivocally for this two
week stretch.

I wrote to close friends
(And they are many)...

"You will be with me on this journey.
Your heart and caring for people will
touch everyone with whom I connect."

It is at the same time,
An expression of Love and
Appreciation for people dear to me.

But it is, at its root, much more.

It is linking souls across continents
and cultures
(It is all the same).

It is sharing harmony in humanity.

I am surrounded by wonderful people.

Returning

February 2001...
The plane was preparing to land in what he
knew then as Saigon,
Now Ho Chi Minh City.

It was a quiet effortless approach
Into a well manicured international airport.

He recalled an earlier time,
An empty pit forming in his stomach.

February 1969...
Bile in his throat,
Trying to hide his shaking from fear
And the feeling of foreboding.

Thup, thup, thup thup...
The blades of the helicopter gun ship
above him, keeping him aloft,
Out of harms way.

Thup, thup, thup, thup...
He fought to stay focused,
His hands steadying the mounted
gattling gun at the open bay door,
Pointed toward the jungle below.

Afraid he would see rustling greenery—
movement below,
And have to shoot to stop it.

To kill the faceless enemy in the brush.
No—admit it. Say it...
Another Human Being.

Later, he would relive it.
Over and over for a dark eternity.
Every night for the rest of his life.

Drenched in sweat,
Sleepless nights.
Safe at home, but unable to speak it,
His shame, his pain from it years earlier.
His unending private grief.

Then, a young man decorated for
his gallantry in war, under fire.
Now, years later, in bed with his wife
beside him asleep,
Trying to hide his sobbings in his pillow.
Whimpering.

Thup, thup, thup, thup...
Nothing gallant preparing to kill from
two hundred feet in the air.
Or for that matter, from anywhere.

Who would, who *could* forgive him?

It was survival.
It was organized war,
He just an insignificant in the middle.

He just obeyed orders,
And for that,
Haunted for his life.

He lived through it (somehow).
He came home.
He was ashamed.

Now he returns,
Trying to right wrongs
of thirty-two years ago.

Hoping for some peace of mind.

The Trek

Day One.

After nearly twenty-six hours of continual travel,
We pull into our hotel and light for a
two minute breather.

No sleep,
No real rest,
But quickly into full clown gear and grease paint.

(I'll unpack later.)

Get prepared to join a Harrier Hash Six K
Run/Walk in the hinterland an hour and
a half bus ride outside Saigon.

Not yet used to the time change nor the heat
and humidity,
We clowns get ready to walk,
To entertain along the route.

And we walked!

Through back semi-jungle paths barely two
feet wide,
At the edge of small back woods villages
and bungalows. (Some actually shacks.)
Near small garden patches for family
consumption.
Along criss-crossing trenched canals filled
with disposed of sewage.

Immediate emersion into another culture.
But, laughs and smiles all the same.

We engage little children, adults and old
folks with our foolery.

We whisk by some, barely a chance for
them to soak in our colors, our gestures,
our laughs.

Most have never seen anything like us or
our antics,
But most laugh and smile outwardly—
Unguarded.

The littlest ones run away in glee, peering
back from behind mammas' skirts or
house pillars,
Then run out again and laugh with us.

Good natured people responding to
self-effacing humor and openness.

We all got it—the message and connections
were clearly made.

Hours later, back in the hotel.
Exhausted.

But grateful for this fulfilling first day.

Little Faces

Day Two.
Saigon.

Today, after a good night's rest,
We clowned at an orphanage for children
with disfigured faces.

From four months to maybe six years old.
About seventy kids in all.

Our photographer took "before"
pictures for Doctors
who will visit in April to
perform corrective surgery.

This is a dreary, darkish place,
Well kept, but old and rundown.
Crowded with children.

The tiniest ones are lined up in rows of cribs,
Seemingly as far as the eye can see.
(I would guess forty or so).
Older kids play in large pens.

Babies most, with baby skin,
Soft but crumpled and
scarred.

This place is a shock to me.
So many little faces,
In a dungeon-like feeling place.

All with some disfigurement
which can affect the rest of
their young lives.

We clown with these little ones.
They take us at face value
(Scary as that sounds).

Their reactions to us reflect love.
Spirit and joy of the young,
In spite of their conditions.

I am in awe watching the staff here.
They are exceptional.
They, too, project love,
Caring for all these children.

We joked with them and embraced
them as much as the children.

All here are delightful,
But the place is oppressive.

(And I am told we have not yet seen real
poverty or harsh conditions.)

Only our second day in-country,
And already I am struck by how well
I live,
What we take for granted.

But more, I am stunned by how much
needs to be done.

These beautiful little faces.

Like A River's Path

It is the end of our second day—
Saigon.

We twenty-seven have been doing
different things,
Some by themselves,
Some in small groups.

But we are flowing in the same direction,
Always.

The undercurrent is the focus to do The
Greater Good,
Each in our own way.

The hotel lobby is an island in our river
At the crossing of our currents.
The crossing of our individual journeys.

We stop for brief respites from the flow here.

But, already, it is more than just
perfunctory "Hello's."

We meet.
A hand caressing a shoulder,
A pat on the back becoming a deeper caring
touch.

To say I am comfortable with these "strangers"
is an understatement.

We are in the same flow of this river,
Bank to bank.

Four To One

We haven't known each other long.

We are four very different people,
Four uniquely identifiable clowns.

But, in two days,
We have bonded.

One, watching the others' backs,
Each of us.

Each sensitive to the others' auras.
Each giving way to the others as we work.

More than courtesy,
More than respect.

It is the caring among us borne from love
for the human spirit.
(A clown universal.)

In two days, uniquely in this time and place,
But now for our life times,
We four have become as one.

Angels On Our Shoulders

There is one among us
With the gift of heavenly connections.

He has engaged the Angels to guide us.

He watches out for all our well-being.

Moment to moment,
He scans the horizon
To ensure we are all safe.

More than just clowning,
More than for the children
we came for and to laugh with.

Greater than any of us.

He beckons the Light
And bathes us in It.

More Yet?

Day Four.

Two clowning events under our belts.

I am experiencing a connection not
experienced before.

As with all things, I believe I was
beckoned to join this troupe,
This Kids First entourage.

We have just started our work.
I have just begun my emersion in Vietnam,
A place and people so foreign to me.

But something deeply profound for me has
already begun to happen.
I am experiencing The Greater Good being
manifested right before my eyes.
Large doses, continuously.

These Kids First people.
Their focus.
Their caring for others of another completely different culture.
Their quiet passion to make a difference.
Their fervor to make things work to conclusions with tangible results.

I can feel the intensity of Grace among them (and I am not a religious person).

It is infectious.
Not talked about, just expressed in actions.
It is magnificent.

And I am told,
"The best is yet to come."

Mr. Hot Air

As with most things in life,
Clowns, too, come in a variety of shapes,
dispositions and sizes.
Well, this one - Safari, is no exception.

Shape—BIG
Disposition—Gloriously happy!
Size—XXXL

Without any doubt,
The rationale for all that he is and does
is Love.

This clown can engage kids with his
boisterousness, belly laughter and
balloonary faster than any clown
I have ever seen!

(And, believe me, I have been
around clowns!)

This clown is a biker, a former
submariner, a computer wizard,
an entrepreneur, and Santa Claus.

More than anything else,
He is driven by Caring.

White face,
Small red heart on the tip of his nose,
Purple curly haired wig, small hat,
Matching violet beard (real beard!),
Multi-colored outfit.

I sat with this hulk of a clown for an hour,
Watching him blow up balloons,
Non-stop.

He blew, I knotted.
He blew, I knotted.

One hundred balloons from his
massive lungs.

Talk about hot air!

And that just the beginning.

His balloon magic is marvelous.

He left a legacy all over the country—
Literally.

Everywhere we were,
There were kids,
There were adults,
Shop keepers,
Policemen,
Street vendors,
Cyclo drivers—Everyone

With Balloon hats,
With Balloon flowers,
With Balloon dogs,
With Balloon swords,

On the streets,
In the shops,
In restaurants,
In our hotels,
Everywhere.

Like it was natural to have them!

And every time I saw his inflated
masterpieces,
I smiled to myself,
Chuckled to myself, and
Thanked Safari for being there.

Thank you, Safari,
Thank you.

What a difference you make!

The Flight To Hue

We left early on Day Five for a one hour
flight from Saigon to Hue.

Organized chaos to the airport.
More luggage for twenty-seven people
than for an entire army.

Scrambling to get organized,
Then waiting on long lines to check-in,
Then rushing to the gate.

Finally aboard and seated.

I was sweaty and uncomfortable,
Cramped shoulder to shoulder between
two others.
The dreaded center seat.

The cold sandwich in front of me,
Unappetizing, as hungry as I was.

I sat and shut out these temporary circumstances,
Instead, reflecting on our journey so far,
Not even a week old.

My eyes wide open, but my head in another dimension.

I thought of the people we were and the people we had met.
I relived the connections we have charged,
And felt them all over, again.

I visualized changed lives
Because of our presence in these moments.

I cried softly,
Grateful for this.
Exhausted and exhilarated.

Contrast

Day Six.
By bus from Hue to Dong Ha Town.

A two hour bumpy drive into the country.

Dilapidated shacks,
Ornate ancestral burial mausoleums
sprinkled around the landscape,
honoring family lineage.

Rich green fields of rice paddies,
Sectored off by irrigation motes.

Oxen immersed in water to their necks
to stay cool.

Rough dirt roads.
Constant honkings and swervings
Among motor bikes and bicycles,
Somehow avoiding multiple collisions.

Cyclo's (bicycle carts), ladened with
inconceivably balanced loads of
everything imaginable.

People working everywhere.
Manual labor.

And we, cutting through this not quite
primitive scenery,
In our modern, air conditioned, not quite
plush bus with padded seats and large
tinted windows.

Peering out at a different culture in their
own land.

An amazing dichotomy,
A stark contrast of "them" and "us."

Them oblivious to us.
(And me, struck by it all.)

Surreal.

MORE Food!

Like Hong Kong, last December.
Marvelous food in this culture.

I have decided to legally change
my name...

Food Boy.

I will only answer to *Food Boy.*

White Reminder

On our drive to Dong Ha,
A landscape of stunted trees
has an eerie look.

If you look closely,
Huge bomb craters, still.
Everywhere.

The ground is earth color, but patched
with white.

I thought, lime?
(Stupid me.)

I am told this area was heavily bombed
and defoliated with toxic chemicals
(Agent Orange and more),
Over thirty years ago.

The trees, although green,
Are small,
New as of five years ago,
But dwarfed.

The white is sand,
Blown in by winds from the ocean beaches
Twenty miles away.

Blown in years ago on to devastated, barren,
And scalped land (and people),
Without green cover to stop it.

Created by war.

Window View

We were stopped in Dong Ha for
just a moment.

Young ladies in coolly hats,
Up to the bus windows,
Selling oranges, other fruit from baskets.

Beautiful smiling faces.
Glistening white teeth.
Smooth skin.

Laughing,
Wordlessly cajoling us to buy.

A warm welcome to us.

Five Red Hearts

Day Six.
February 21, 2001.

The Kids First School
Awards Ceremony,
Dong Ha.

Many many people at this function.

We four clowns had done our thing,
Run into the main area doing clown antics
for all the kids.
Made a quick exit, then, so the ceremonies
could continue.

We sequestered ourselves out of view,
in the Kids First bus,
Not wanting to disrupt the proceedings,

Peering out from behind the drawn window
curtains,
Catching glimpses of it all.

We saw and heard the awarding of
scholarships to timid but proud children,
All dressed in the same school uniforms.

Then, six prosthetic legs and one arm,
Each to a small child.

A knock on the bus door,
A request for Safari to join on stage.

It was then I was told he had arranged for
five tailor-made wheel chairs to be
given to kids, today.

I watched through the glass as Safari
walked up on the stage.

This was a different moment for him.
(And for us.)

Although in full clown paint and garb,
A moment beyond clowning.
(Or maybe an extension of it.)

Behind his grease paint, obviously
moved and emotional.

This was another of his contributions,
But with different effect.
Longer lasting effect.
Tangible.

I saw him give a short speech,
Although I could not hear his words.

Each of the five chairs moved from the
stage side into position,
Un-owned for just a brief moment more.

One by one, a limbless small child placed
into each.

And then, without a word,
This massive clown reached inside his clown pocket,
Pulled out and blew up a single red heart balloon,
And handed it to the first of these children.

Then, silently (but deftly),
Repeated four times more.

We three in the bus looked at each other,
But could say nothing.

One Red Heart—Revisited

The Kids First School
Awards Ceremony,
Dong Ha.

This day was almost more than I could take.

The emotion was overpowering.

We were all on the bus, ready to head back to the hotel,
The four of us still shaken from everything that went on.
Our faces on the school through the bus windows.

As the bus slowly pulled into motion,
I saw the small boy in his new wheel chair, with determination,
Pushing the wheels over the dirt and gravel school yard toward us leaving.

His mother walked slowly beside him, watching him,
The red heart balloon pinched between her two fingers.

Mobile for the first time in his life.
Mobile for the rest of his life.
New horizons.

They saw us moving out, and looked up.
Looked directly at Safari.

The Rush

We are somewhere mid-trip,
And I have begun to get the sensation

...That there is not much time left.

...That there is so much to do,

Here...and everywhere

To repair lives from whatever
devastation has crushed,
disabled or derailed people.

The degree of hurt doesn't
matter.

The country,
The circumstances,
The nature of the chaos that caused
the imbalances of lives...
...None of it matters.

I feel that we are rushing down out-moded,
ill-equipped roads that can barely take
the weight of our sophisticated
high tech vehicle.

It is as if we are geared to move at warp
speed,
But we are in slow motion.

Trying to beat the eventuality of the
destruction of lives.

We need to move faster!

We need to do more
in the World!

WE NEED TO BAND TOGETHER!

WE NEED EACH OTHER
TO HELP EACH OTHER....

...TO HELP ALL OF US.

Oh, To Fly!

(February 22, 2001—
The Ground Breaking Ceremony
of Friendship Village, Dong Ha
sponsored by Peace Trees Vietnam)

I am on the sidelines, just a spectator.
Watching this ceremony.

This village will be home for people
who can't afford much on their own.
Those who are disadvantaged and coping
with lasting challenges yet from
"The Conflict."

Approximately one hundred homes for
several hundred people.

Assembled under a large blue canopy
shielding from the hot sun,
Provincial officials, Peace Trees members,
workers, villagers, US embassy people,
others of us on-lookers.

Listening to the speeches.
Impassioned words.
Visions of things better—to be in this village.

Vietnamese and Americans together pick up
large decorated shovels.
With ceremony, in unison they shovel the
first clumps of earth toward rebuilding a
community of lives through this village to be.

This is a moment in time, a nano-second
in the continuum.
But it is life changing for the people
developing this village,
For those who will call this place home, and
For others of us on the fringes watching.

On the broad scale, projects like this
are insignificant—
And yet they are *the most* significant.

They are a testament to people's true nature,
I believe, to want to care for others.
Everything I see here are
efforts to rebuild lives.

If you were not here, you missed this one.

I pray these things are happening as
little bursts of Love and energy worldwide,
But I am not sure there are enough of them.

I wish I could fly at light speed,
Visiting these instances of human connections
around the world as they happen.

I would harvest the intent, the dedication,
the passion of people for people.
I would seed them to grow forests of Love
among us to blanket the earth.

Oh, I wish I could fly.

Dear Kay

(To my long time friend Kay Williams,
who suggested Kids First apply for a
Boeing grant to support the Kids First
Rehabilitation Vocational Village
development)

I wish you were here!

It is your style.
It has your aura here.
It is all about helping others—as you are.

At this moment, as I listen to the speeches
about the promise and vision for this
place,
I feel you with me.

You are here with me, Kay.

(I just needed to tell you,
even though I know you know it.)

Trees Of Peace

Outside Dong Ha,
There is what used to be a
U.S. Marine base.

On the site, now,

Sits the Dannan Parry Land Mine
Education Center,
Built in 1998.

The Center is in the midst of
rows and rows of trees,
About seventeen hundred,
Almost a forest.
Lush greenery.

Planted in 1996.

Forty-three Americans,
Forty-three Vietnamese,
Almost four weeks,
Together.

Inch by inch, painstakingly,
The land first cleared of ordnances
By Vietnamese trained in this dangerous work.

Below many,
Memorabilia of soldiers gone
from the war.

Purple Hearts,
Combat Ribbons,
Dog Tags,
Military Citations,
Notes,
Letters,
Poems.

As each tree was planted.
Poems and notes were read.

A moment of silence observed.

A living memorial.

Trees of Peace.

The Second Ground Breaking

(February 23, 2001—
The Ground Breaking Ceremony
of The Rehabilitation and Vocational
Training Village, Dong Ha
sponsored by Kids First)

The second ceremony.

The set up same as the last only
more elaborate.
School band, more flowers, more dancers
and all.

I was stirred by the Peace Trees Village
Ceremony the day before,
But this is more intense.
This is more meaningful to me.

The huge brightly lettered backdrop says.
"sponsored by Kids First."
This sinks in—differently than yesterday.

I am not just a spectator here.

I have read the proposal for this village.
(I was in awe of its scope and
comprehensiveness).

I have spoken at length with Roger about
this vision.

I have been with him in his request for
grant money.

I have committed to Arden and Roger my
support of their causes.

I know these people. I am with them, as
one of the Kids First group here.

I am sitting behind Arden and Roger,
two rows back under the canopy.
They in the front row, more well dressed
for this than the rest of us.

They look quietly proud and
professionally calm.
But I know them some.

Their emotions are high.
They are front and center in this.
I sense them struggling
to keep their demeanor.
This is the fruition of their vision
long in planning.

I am overwhelmed by this,
By them—these two, and what they
continue to accomplish for other people.

They ask nothing for themselves.
(More reason I am with them.)

I see the backs of their heads,
Us all listening to other speakers
before it is Roger's turn.

Now, at the podium, Roger speaks of
this village,
This dream beginning.

I can see the easels to Roger's left with
architectural rendering of the
finished setting.

And, Roger continues...
Words not about him or Arden, or
Kids First,
But *about their gratefulness for the
opportunity to contribute!*

Roger finishes to loud applause, thanking
the people of Quang Tri Province and
Dong Ha Town for allowing Kids First
to be here.

I can hardly help but cry.
I am humbled to be with these people,
These Kids First people.

So much more than a name,
A quiet statement and passion
of commitment...

Kids First.

Appreciate—
But With Caution

The setting for this well planned Kids First
Rehabilitation Vocational Training Village
is a beautiful fifty acre site.

It is lush green with trees and fields,
A calming reservoir lake,
Serene.
So peaceful.

A so appropriate setting for rebuilding lives.

And yet, we have been cautioned...

DO NOT STRAY FROM THIS SMALL
COMMON CLEARED AREA!

STAY ON THE WELL BEATEN ROAD!

The entire site—just beyond the ground
breaking ceremony area has yet to be cleared
of unexploded ordnances.

The serenity of hope for this land is deceiving.
We must be on guard, still—thirty-five years
later.

I have to think about this contrast...
I have to think about this.

The Rules

Day Seven.
Friday.
February 23, 2001.

Earlier, Ground Breaking for the Kids First
Rehabilitation Vocational Village,
Then lunch with dignitaries and all.

Now, an hour drive back to Hue,
The day's festivities completed.

Time on the bus to reflect, to quietly renew,
and to rewind emotions,
Time to think.

But, no-o-o!

First Arden, then Nancy, then Peggy,
then Carol, then me.

(I, the butt of it all, and gladly for these
Ladies.)

Jabber, jabber, jabber.

Six Rules For Men!

What?
What men do that women laugh at,
they explain to me almost in unison.

Who knew??

A sentence,
A rule.
Laughter,
Rule revision.

A sentence.
A rule.
More laughter.

What cheerios?
What sponge battle ships?
What is with this?

It is a different use of the English language.
New meanings,
New vernacular.

We laugh,
Then laugh again,
More and more.

The list grew to eight rules,
then quickly to ten,

Finally (I think) twelve.

No, I can't repeat them here.
There may be children and grand parents
reading this.

We all howled, and loved it.

I Have Figured You Out!

Okay, Roger,
I finally have it!
(Not that you would tell me.)

Until I arrived here in Vietnam,
I kept asking myself...What *will*
all the rest of these people with
Kids First do here?

Is this just a tour?
(Although, you, Roger would deny that.)

Besides the core group of Kids First
And us clown "hangers-on,"
Why are these other people here?

But, now I know.

Your goal, Roger,
(And don't even try to hide it!)
Is Kids First support
And much more.

I know you want people to support your causes,
But in a way, I also think you don't care about that.

Like the others close to you,
You are focused to do The Greater
Good in the world,
In Vietnam and beyond.

So, here is my conclusion.
(You sly fox, you.)

(And I know I am right!)

You plan these excursions
To expose others to The Gift of Giving.

You guide people to places and experiences
Where they can decide for themselves
What is meaningful to them,
What "feels" good and fulfilling,
Where they want to contribute beyond
themselves.

I believe you are a visionary.
The work you do is incredible.

But, in truth,
You are a messenger.

(And, I *know* I am right!)

One Spoon At A Time

Day Eight.
We are on the Perfume River out of Hue,
A "tour" boat of sorts,
Chugging toward the South China Sea.

Our destination a small remote village
To give a water buffalo for farming.

Relaxing and chatting in small groups,
Marveling at the river sights,
Catching up with each other's lives.

Scooter and I talk.
We get to favorite stories in our pasts.

Scooter says,
High school in California,
His clique of twelve friends.

Musing one day ...
All the poster pictures of hungry children
seem to show forks and knives, but
No spoons.

"This is wrong!" they say.

(High school kids talk about
strange things).

A pact is made among them.
Fix this imbalance!

Over six months, Scooter continues,
Each quietly "borrows" cafeteria spoons,
One-at-a-time.

In one fell swoop.
Amazement at C.A.R.E.
Five hundred spoons show up
anonymously.

Peace returns to these youth.

Lam Phan

Lam is a Vietnamese American lawyer.
Left years ago at the last moment.
With almost nothing.

Rebuilt his life,
And now returns to rebuild in his
homeland.
A core member of Kids First.

At first appearances,
Lam is reserved.
(But he will fool you.)

Below the surface, quick witted,
An intellect with endurance,
Sincere and passionate.

From our first meeting, months ago,
From our brief chat on a ferry to Seattle,
I knew we were connected.

I felt it in his eyes,
Heard it in his voice,
Still do.

We joke with each other,
At the other's expense,
As only open, trusting souls do.

On the Perfume River,
We shared steamed crab together,
Both of us nose to nose bent over a
common bowl,
Crab muck on our faces and fingers.

It was an unspoken special connection
to both of us,
Our private "toast" to each other, together.

UUFADA—FUUFADA

Day Ten.
On our two buses.
Five hour drive south from Hue to Hoi An.

(It would be another one of *those* days.)

We are all rummy at 8:15 a.m.

Yikes! Four hours and forty five minutes
stuck on this bus with these crazy people.

It takes us all of ten minutes to start laughing
and telling the worst jokes anybody could
think of.

But, we are the best of the two bus loads,
And we know it.
And, we will tell anybody we are!
(Except the other bus load.)

Rummy, rummy, rummy.
Bad joke, bad joke, bad joke.
But we howl at all of them.

(At least, so far, no one has gas.)

Throughout, in the background of
our childish insanity,
I hear the bus horn...raspy.
Straining each time to get its sound out...

UUFADA - FUUFADA,
FUUFADA - UUFADA.

I am struck absolutely dumb with laughter.

Swerving here, dodging there.
The only thing saving us from Creamed
Corn of Motor Bike is.....

UUFADA - FUUFADA
FUUFADA - UUFADA.

Who could seriously take that as a warning?

This must be the only bus in the world with
this horn!

UUFADA - FUUFADA...

It is a clown horn disguised as a bus
If I ever heard one!

FUUFADA - UUFADA,
UUFADA - FUUFADA.

I am laughing so hard,
There are tears running down my face.

Where am I?
Who are these people?

How could we ever explain this if
we hit something???

Cultivate Caring

I have not before visited a “third world”
country.

The sights are different than I know,
the customs as well,
Much new to me.

Sounds, smells, tastes,
All foreign to me.

Technology as I know it,
Sparse in many areas.

Farming is with oxen and human hand.
Mostly manual labor.

People subsist on little,
Doing small jobs to live meager existences
(At least by my lifestyle).

But, as I am witnessing this,
The spirit of people is a constant.

It is what I know from where I come.

Especially the children.

The children,
Oh, the children!

Yes, the children!
Treasures to nurture and cultivate.

They will make the difference for all our futures.

We owe them the care to blossom beyond our mistakes and frailties.

Not History To My Eyes

The Citadel in Hue.
Home to Vietnamese imperial dynasties.
An ancient walled city.

Today, a park,
A veritable playground.
Playing fields, souvenir stands
among temple relics.

And, in a corner,
A small open air grave yard.

On cement slabs,
U.S. tanks and weaponry,
All on display.

Relics from "the conflict."
Paraded before me by the victors.

Rusted by weather and time,
Blood and terror long since washed away.

Each with similar plaques,
"U.S. equipment of the 8th Army,
used by "Puppet Soldiers"
(the South Vietnamese Army),
captured March 1975 at ..."

I touched the metal.
Cold in the warm sunlight,
Even now.

Uncertain emotions surfaced—surged.

"The Conflict" we called it.

Almost sixty thousand of us,
Over three million of them.
Dreams never fulfilled on all sides.

Unlike World War Two.
Unlike the Korean War.
This was not my father's war.

I almost went.

I lost friends,
Had some return.
Some physically maimed,
All emotionally scarred.

Several with us now
were here then.

This is not history to me.
This is not history to me.

Parallels

Hanoi.
Mason Centralle,
The Hanoi Hilton.

Now a museum.

I went reluctantly,
Just knowing its focus would be
about imprisoned and tortured
American pilots.
All about "us."

(What else *could* it be about?)

It was not at all what I expected.

The story of American pilots was told
in a seven-by-seven foot room.
Small in comparison to this once massive hell.

The suffering of Americans here not to be
diminished,
But our presence in Vietnam a mere blip on
Vietnam's historical radar screen.

This was a prison to many from 1856.
Vietnamese ideologists and dissidents.

Pages and pages of books and books of
Vietnamese faces,
Incarcerated here,
Tortured here,
Murdered here.

Occupation of a gentle people with grand
visions.
Suppressed
By the Chinese,
By the French,
By the Japanese.

From the tools displayed,
All masters of torture.

In fear of people with dreams
For their own kind in their own land.

This is reminiscent of another continent,
Another conflict,
Another time.

It is of my brother Joseph.
South Africa.
1969-1994.
Robins Island.
Another prison.

But the same ideologists,
And the same fears of their vision.

In solitary confinement,
Tortured,
Months and years at a time.

I understand the fear of the vision of others,
I understand the need to survive.

But it is no less painful to consider
Humans suffering at the hands of humans.

Tragedy.
All of it.

There can be so much more.
There *is* so much more.

The Truth

It would appear that the "truth" is that
of the teller.

The North Vietnamese say the truth
is the South Vietnamese were
"Puppet Soldiers,"
Forced to fight supporting the U.S. troops.

Our truth was we didn't lose "the conflict,"
We just decided to pull out.

In Vietnam this trip, from "propaganda"
I saw,
The truth is what the victor of the war
says it is.

Others say the truth is somewhere between
what opposing sides say it is.

Now, I will tell you the Truth.

The Truth is that the only way things change
for the better is that caring people extend
themselves to help others.

The Truth is we all need to be needed and
cared for somehow.

The Truth is—deep down and unspoken
for some, and on the surface for others—
We all feel other people's sufferings and
tragedies.

The Truth is we all appreciate others who
care and who do something about caring
for others.

The Truth is we can only make it
If we discard (no, more than that—forgive)
historical mistakes,
And embrace each other in Humanity.

The Truth is each of us knows something
or someone or has something
That can make *the* positive difference for
someone else's life.
(And the Truth is it doesn't take much, either.)

I am done with this subject, for now.

But you get the picture...
Live The Truth.

The Last Show

Our last night in Vietnam.
Hanoi.

Our last meal as a group.
Heartfelt spoken appreciations and
impromptu comments,
A celebration of a new group
Coalesced in two weeks.

Afterwards, Rags (our group photographer),
Safari and I
To the little boot shop to pick up
our custom made clown shoes.
Not quite done.

The boot maker worked, the rest of us
in a circle on the floor,
Three generations of family,
Boot maker off to the side,
sewing our shoes.

We sat two hours on small stools
in this tiny street front shop.

No costumes,
No grease paint.
Just balloons and laughter.
And one red nose.

We spoke no intelligible words,
None of them English.
We no Vietnamese.

But, how we communicated!

Grandpa, Grandma,
Sons, wives, daughters,
And seven children.

Twelve of us packed into
this little shop.

That red nose flew from face to face,
And each time it landed,
A new funny look mimed by the
wearer to us all.
Around and around it went.

Balloons sprung up in various shapes.
A hat for Grandpa,
A flower for a little daughter,
A sword for a little grandson.

Then, motions of announcement.
Shoes were done!

Placed on my feet,
Modeled for the "crowd."

I bowed to the boot maker,
He the same in return.

Claps and howls from the group,
us all still on the floor.

Then, like the nose,
The shoes made the rounds.

The littlest ones got lost in the red and
blue leather,
Stood, wobbled, fell over and laughed.

Grandma in these huge shoes
and red nose,
Posed for pictures.

Thank you's to all,
Hugs and kisses.

A fitting last show.

Hong Kong And Home

End of this trip.
From Hanoi to Hong Kong.

I left the group to stay in Hong Kong
with friends for three more days.

When arranged, I told them,
"Seeing you so soon,
Icing on this delicious cake of a trip."

We first connected three months earlier
in Hong Kong.
Then, too, as their guest.
Then, too, clowning for children's schools
and orphanages.

Immediate connection together.
More laughter than ten people deserve in
a life.

They wined me.
They dined me.
They were at my beck and call.
(Although they would deny it
to my face.)
All the while they making fun of me,
and me of them.

Always prodding, always cajoling,
Side long looks waiting for returned barbs.

Eyes twinkling.
Bursts of belly laughter.
What great times!

(Friendships can be exhausting.)

I was invited in with their clan.
Their close, long time friends,
More of the same.

Evelyn, Ken, Doug.
I love these people.

(Writing this now, I am laughing
out loud at our antics and
the thought of us together.)

Then, preparing to leave, again.

Such conflict.
Always the same.
Leaving and wanting to go home.
Yearning to see my wife,
And hating to leave this trio
and their groupies.

A strange mix of emotions.
Leaving and returning
all at once.

(I can't wait to host them at our home.)

I have enormous wealth.

Home

I am home, now.

Familiar surroundings I love.
Comfortable to my lifestyle.

Seeing people I have known and
loved forever.

Getting back into my own routine.

But, I sit frequently, musing.
Eyes closed,
Recalling the sights and sounds,
The smells, the people on this just
concluded journey.

New friends made,
Old ones visited.

Caring expressed risk free and returned
through our eyes from our hearts.

Verbal language never a barrier.

Openness.
Giving to give,
No strings attached.

I can taste every tear of joy down
my cheek.

This two weeks plus,
Just a speck on the map,
But meaningful beyond expression.

Deep connections made will grow deeper
and wider,
With all our continuing nurturing.

Conclusion

If you have ever thought about giving—in any manner, in any degree, for any cause or people you feel are worthwhile, do it.

Do it now.

It is the definition of Life itself.

It creates infectious joy and love.

It breeds "caring for" at its foundation.

Be part of the Universe.
Give yourself away to others.

You will reap unbelievable riches from not wanting them.

About the Author

In addition to being a writer, Jed is cofounder of *The Institute for Personal and Professional Effectiveness* (IPPE). The Institute was established out of a sincere desire to improve the personal and professional lives of a broad spectrum of people.

Throughout his thirty-six years in business, Jed has been a vocal advocate for progressive employee empowerment. He believes respecting and dignifying people as "whole persons" is an essential cornerstone to lasting business success.

He is a proponent of the philosophy that attracting, developing and retaining the most competent workforce is a key business success factor, and is dependent on providing a work environment in which employees can be professionally and personally fulfilled.

Jed is a former twenty-seven year career executive with a global Fortune 50 company. He held senior level management positions in the areas of intellectual property protection, computing security, and uniformed security and fire protection responsible for worldwide support to major operating organizations for these functions. His experience and accomplishments encompass success in managing large and small professional as well as unionized work groups and leadership of innovative and culture changing projects.

Jed has led national security initiatives and represented industry associations in resolving security policy issues with numerous government agencies and the White House.

Throughout his career, Jed has been a guest and keynote speaker at forums and seminars on the topics of motivation, leadership, and effective management, in addition to topics on intellectual property protection and computing security.

Jed and his wife of thirty-one years live in Bellevue, Washington.

Their twenty-five-year-old son is a professional guitarist in New York City. Their twenty-four-year-old daughter is a freelance writer and music/film critic in Portland, Oregon.

You may contact Jed through the IPPE web site:
http://www.ippe.com

or directly via his email address:
selter@ippe.com

Order Form

QTY.		Price	Can. Price	Total
	Behind the Grease Paint— A Clown's Chronicle in Vietnam -Jed "Duffy" Selter	$11.95	$15.95 CN	
	Shipping and Handling Add $3.50 for orders in the US/Add $7.50 for Global Priority			
	Sales tax (WA state residents only, add 8.8%)			
	Total enclosed			

Telephone Orders:
Call 1-800-461-1931
Have your VISA or
MasterCard ready.

Fax Orders:
425-398-1380
Fill out this order form and fax.

Postal Orders:
Hara Publishing
P.O. Box 19732
Seattle, WA 98109

E-mail Orders:
harapub@foxinternet.net

Method of Payment:

☐ Check or Money Order

☐ VISA

☐ MasterCard

Expiration Date: ______________

Card #: ______________________

Signature: ____________________

Name ____________________________________
Address __________________________________
City ____________________ State _____ Zip ________
Phone (   ) ______________ Fax (   ) __________

Call 425-398-3679 for more information.
Thank you for your order!